D.J.'s

FULL HOUSE

FLIP~OVER BOOK

D.J.'s

FULL HOUSE

FLIP~OVER BOOK

By Devra Speregen

A Creative Media Applications Production

SCHOLASTIC INC.
New York Toronto London Auckland Sydney

ISBN 0-590-20257-X

12 11 10 9 8 7 6 5 4 3   4 5 6 7 8 9/9

Printed in the U.S.A.   40

First Scholastic printing, November 1994

DJ

It took me over an hour to get out of the house this afternoon.

First of all, I couldn't find a thing to wear. I was planning on wearing my khaki overalls skirt with a black bodysuit underneath, but I couldn't find the bodysuit anywhere. I have a hunch on where it is though. I'll have to remember to check Stephanie's closet when I get home.

Then, just when I was ready to leave, Dad came into my room, insisting on putting shelf paper on the shelves in my closet. So I had to take everything off the shelves and put it all on my bed until he was finished. That took a good half hour.

But the hardest part was trying to sneak out the front door with Joey, Uncle Jesse, Aunt Becky, Nicky, Alex, and Michelle right there in the living room, watching a video. I had to wait until Michelle got hungry and they all went into the kitchen for lunch.

So here I am in downtown San Francisco, sitting in an office building, waiting to be interviewed. Kimmy dropped me off on the way to her dentist's appointment. I would have driven here myself, but Dad grounded me from using the car for the weekend because he found out I was driving without any wiper fluid.

"How are you going to clean your windshield without any fluid?" he'd asked me.

It's not really a major big deal, but if you knew my dad and how important cleanliness is to him, you'd understand.

Anyway, I'm trying to keep this interview a secret. You see, I've entered our family in a contest for Family of the Year. That's where I am now, at contest headquarters, waiting to be interviewed by the judges. I heard about the contest a couple of weeks ago. There was a huge poster on the window of Make-up Mart at the mall. My best friend, Kimmy, and I were there buying a new tube of Pleasing Pink Petunia lipstick for Kimmy when I saw it.

It read:

DO YOU COME FROM A BIG, HAPPY FAMILY?

I totally freaked out.

Do you think your big, happy family has what it takes to be Golden Gate's Big, Happy Family of the Year?

Big, Happy Family of the Year. Now does *my* family qualify for that, or what?

I grabbed an entry form and stuffed it into my pocket. I wanted to enter and keep it a secret from my family. Then they'd be *really* surprised if we won. Boy, it would be a blast if we did.

The Grand Prize is a huge San Francisco shopping spree, a family portrait taken on a San Francisco cable car, a tour of the Ghirardelli chocolate factory (Michelle would love that), and a guest appearance on the TV show, *San Francisco Beat*. I've had a crush on Kyle Kravitz, the host of that show, for years. If we win, I'll get to meet him!

Anyway, the entry form was super long and since I had *so* much spare time with my six million hours of homework, it took forever to fill out. But they must have liked what I wrote, because they called me to come in for this interview.

So here I am, sitting on a bench in the hallway, waiting for a Mr. Fabres and a Ms. Newman to ask me about the Tanners. I hope the denim skirt and sweater I ended up wearing is okay.

I wonder what's taking so long? I hope the interview doesn't take forever. I have to get back home before Dad realizes I'm not in my room reorganizing my closet.

•　　•　　•　　•　　•　　•

Big, Happy
Family of the Year

Contestant Family: _The Tanner Family_

Name of Applicant: _Donna Jo (D.J.) Tanner_

Address: _1882 Girard Street_

San Francisco, CA

CONTESTANT FAMILY

Please list all family members, their occupations, and relationship to applicant.

Name	Occupation	Relationship
1. Danny Tanner	TV Talk Show Co-Host	Father
2. Donna Jo Tanner	High School Senior	
3. Stephanie Tanner	Seventh-Grade Student	Sister
4. Michelle Tanner	Third-Grade Student	Sister
5. Jesse Katsopolis	Radio Talk Show Host *	Uncle
6. Rebecca Donaldson Katsopolis	TV Talk Show Co-Host	Aunt
7.+8. Nicholas + Alexander Katsopolis	Preschool Students	Cousins
9. Joseph Gladstone	Radio Talk Show Host + Stand-Up Comedian	Friend

* Also owns the Smash Club

APPLICANT'S PERSONAL INFORMATION

Name: _Donna Jo (D.J.) Tanner_

Hair color: _blond_

Eye color: _blue_

Level of education: _High School Senior_

PLEASE ANSWER THE FOLLOWING QUESTIONS ABOUT YOUR

FAMILY TO THE BEST OF YOUR ABILITY.

1. Why do you feel your family should be nominated as Golden Gate's Big, Happy Family of the Year? _Two reasons. First, because my family is very big and very happy! Even when we fight, we're still happy. Wait, I didn't mean to write that, but I can't erase it now because I wrote it in pen. What I'm trying to say, is that even though we may argue_

occasionally, we're still a happy, loving family. The second reason is that everyone in my family is involved in our community. Danny Tanner, my father, is the host of "Wake Up, San Francisco" along with my Aunt Rebecca. They have very important people on their show and they talk about serious issues. Adam Buffet from "A Greener San Francisco" came on and spoke about recycling. And the mayor helped my dad's network raise money for homeless people. Joey plays in an annual hockey game for charity, and my little sisters, Stephanie and Michelle, are also involved in the community. Uncle Jesse took them to a homeless shelter last year to help serve Christmas dinner. As for me, I volunteer in the Adopt-a-Grand-parent program at a local nursing home every year.

2. What exciting things does your family do together? We take a lot of trips together. We've been to Hawaii, New York, Lake Tahoe and Las Vegas. Last year, we all went to Disney World and this year, Dad says he wants our Tanner Family Vacation to be the most exciting ever. He won't tell us where we're going though because he wants it to be a surprise. Another exciting thing we did together was appear on stage in concert with the Beach Boys. It happened a few years ago. I won this "Dream Night With the Beach Boys," and they came to my house, met my family, and invited us to their concert! That was amazing. My dad has this thing about doing stuff together as a family. He's the founder of Tanner Family

Fun Night (which is not always so fun) and Tanner Family Clean-up Day, which is really only exciting for him since his hobby is cleaning. We also have a Tanner Family Barbecue and a Tanner Family Picnic every year. Our van broke down on the way to the picnic two years ago and we were stuck in the car together for hours. That wasn't so exciting.

3. How do the members of your family get along? This is tough to answer. I say that because for the most part, about ninety-three percent of the time, we get along great. But then there's that seven percent of the time where we get on each other's nerves. But isn't that the way it is with all families? When we do fight, we always make up. Our dad raised us to be very caring and helpful to others. In fact, his motto — "Do unto others as you would have them do unto you, but always clean up afterwards" — is written above the sink in all our bathrooms. And it's true, whenever one of us gets in a bind, there's always eight other people around to help out. Stephanie and I

help out by baby-sitting for Michelle, Nicky, and Alex. And when we were younger, Joey and Uncle Jesse used to baby-sit for us all the time. That was really a sight to see — Uncle Jesse and Joey changing Michelle's diaper!

4. What makes your family big and happy? _What makes us big? Well, there are nine people and a dog living under one roof in my house. I'd call that big! What makes us happy? Just being together makes us happy. We're very happy. Extremely happy. And if we win this contest, we'll be even happier._

5. List three good things about having a big, happy family:

1) _There's always someone around._

2) _We have a ready-made softball team._

3) _My turn to clear the dinner table doesn't come up very often._

and three bad things:

1) _Never enough bathrooms._

2) _____

3) _____

DJ

The Interview

Donna Jo, it's so nice to meet you. Won't you sit down?

Thank you. And you can call me D.J. Everybody does.

Okay, D.J. I'm Michael Fabres and this is Shirley Newman. We are the judges for the Golden Gate's Big, Happy Family of the Year Contest. We'd just like to talk with you a bit, and find out more about your family.

No problem.

I see on your entry form that you're the big sister in your family.

That's right.

What's that like?

Sometimes it's rough, because I always have to set the

example for my younger sisters, Stephanie and Michelle. And it's not fair when Dad lets them get away with things I never would have gotten away with!

What do you mean?

Well, once Stephanie, she's thirteen, let my friend Kimmy pierce her ears, even after Dad said she couldn't until she was in junior high. That's how long I had to wait to get my ears pierced. But Stephanie pierced them anyway and didn't even get grounded.

And then there's Michelle, my youngest sister. She's adorable and sweet, but she always gets away with everything. Once, the three of us were playing around, having a pillow fight, and we accidentally broke a window. Steph and I had to apologize, pay for a new window, and we were grounded for a whole week. Michelle, on the other hand, didn't get so much as a lecture.

So, you don't like being the oldest?

No, most of the time being the big sister is great. Stephanie and Michelle sort of look up to me. Sometimes, they even dress like me! That doesn't bother me, unless, of course, they borrow my clothes without asking and get mustard on them.

Mustard?

Mustard. It doesn't come out of wool, you know. Anyway, I don't let it get to me too much. I know it's a big responsibility being the oldest.

One thing I always make sure of is that I'm there for Stephanie and Michelle. Our mom died when I was ten. Sometimes it's hard on me, not having a mom around, but I know it's hard on my sisters, too. So I try to take care of them the best I can. When Mom died, my uncle Jesse and Joey came to live with us. They've been helping my dad raise us for the past seven years.

Do you think your father will ever get remarried?

I hope so. He came pretty close. He and Vicky were engaged for a while, but she got this great job in New York and they had to break off their engagement. It was so sad when they broke up. We all liked her a lot. Michelle was really bummed about it. She was hoping for a new mother. She even tried to fix him up with her preschool teacher, Miss Wiltrout. She invited Miss Wiltrout over for lunch and served them peanut butter and jelly sandwiches by candlelight. Luckily my dad caught on before the scene got too embarrassing.

Describe your father, Danny Tanner.

There's nobody in the world like my father. He's the most loving, caring, handsome, clean man in the world. You're laughing, but I'm dead serious. We're talking serious clean here. We're talking "I'm ironing my socks so they'll stay fresh and unwrinkled" clean. He's obsessed with it — it's his favorite pastime. He cleans when he's happy, when he's sad . . . he'll use any excuse to clean. How many kids can say their fathers followed them to kindergarten every Monday to scrub and disinfect their nap mats?

None, I'm sure.

But really, my dad is the best. Just a few months ago, a funny thing happened. My dad and I both had dates and we ended up at the same restaurant! It was awkward at

first, but then, when our dates left with each other —
don't ask — we had this really great Father/Daughter talk.
He's finally beginning to treat me like an adult. Well, he
still insists on tucking me in at night, but I know it's just
hard for him to let go. And to tell you the truth, I like
being tucked in.

Go on.

I love my dad very much. He does a lot for us kids. Even
though he works long hours, he still finds time for us.
Once, when I was younger, Dad was working so hard, he
missed my school play and Stephanie's science fair in the
same week. He felt terrible. But I told him not to worry. I
know that he tries to be the best father he can. And he's a
fair dad, too. I got a speeding ticket and tried to hide it
from him. When he found out, he didn't freak like I
thought he would. He grounded me, but he didn't, like,
explode or anything.

I also got a "slowing" ticket once, and that was totally
Dad's fault.

A slowing ticket?

Uh-huh. You see, Dad's a little *overprotective* at times. Especially when it comes to my driving. It happened when he finally let me drive the car on the highway. He sat next to me in the passenger seat, watching me like a hawk. He kept telling me to drive slower and switch into the right, more "sensible," lane. Anyway, I finally got pulled over for driving too slow.

You know what bugs me though? For some unknown reason, my dad is always right. Always! I mean, even when I'm absolutely sure he doesn't know what he's talking about, it always turns out that he was right. It drives me nuts.

One time I got a part-time job as a photographer's assistant at the mall so I could make some extra money to buy these really great sneakers. It was a totally dorky job — I had to dress up like a clown with a big red nose and enormous shoes and try to make little kids laugh, but hey, it was a job. Anyway, Dad didn't want me to work because he thought my schoolwork would suffer. I told him he was crazy and that I was mature enough to handle a job and my schoolwork. And sure enough, I failed a science test a week later because I couldn't find time to study. Right again! Luckily, he was totally cool about it. I mean, yeah, I got grounded for that, too, but, as they say, I learned a valuable lesson. I think.

Well, at least he didn't say, "I told you so."

Should I keep talking?

If you want.

Well, I have one more thing to say about my dad. He can be the absolute coolest sometimes. There was a time that I begged him to trust me and I blew it. My old boyfriend, Steve — we went out for two years but broke up because we weren't connecting anymore — had just moved into his own apartment. Dad thought I was too young to go there at first and we had a huge fight about it. Then, after weeks of begging and pleading with him, he finally agreed to trust me and let me go. And wouldn't you know it, Steve and I fell asleep on his sofa watching television and I missed my curfew! Wow, Dad nearly hit the roof, he was so mad. But when he cooled down, he realized that I had made an honest mistake. He forgave me and — would you believe it — he didn't ground me at all!

Describe your sister Stephanie.

Stephanie Tanner. Stephanie Tanner can be the sweetest, kindest, most adorable kid on the planet. But she can also be the most irritating, infuriating, obnoxious little sister around!

I used to share a room with Stephanie, up until the time I started high school. Then I moved into Michelle's room and Michelle moved in with Stephanie. Stephanie drove me crazy when we lived together. She helped herself to my stuff all the time and I never had any privacy at all. There was even a time when she followed me around, dressing and talking exactly like me. I came this close to taping her mouth shut.

But now I have my own room, and I think she's finally learning to respect my privacy and my things. And except for that one unfortunate mustard incident, we've been getting along much better.

Can you tell us about the "mustard incident"?

Yeah, sure. Stephanie asked if she could borrow one of my new sweaters and I said no. But she took the sweater from my closet and wore it anyway. Now that wouldn't have been so bad — I could have forgiven her for that. But then she accidentally squirted mustard all over it, and tried to wash it.

In the washing machine?

Yup. And guess what? It shrunk down to Michelle's size.

You must have been angry.

I was! Wouldn't you have been? But, uh, wait a sec. This isn't going to ruin the contest for us, is it? I mean, it happened a long time ago, and —

Don't worry. We won't hold it against her.

Thanks. She really is a good sister, I swear. She just gets herself into all these crazy situations. It's like she can't help it — trouble just seems to follow her around. You wouldn't believe me if I told you some of the things that have happened to that sister of mine. But it would take days. Weeks!

How about giving us an example?

An example? Sure. How about this for unbelievable —

when Stephanie was ten years old she drove Joey's car through our kitchen.

Through . . . the . . . kitchen?

Yup, right through the kitchen wall. Pretty wild, huh? Broke right through the wall, the cabinets, everything. And Dad gets on *my* case about my driving! And there's the time Steph won a *hundred thousand dollars* gambling in Lake Tahoe! But good ol' Dad wouldn't let us keep the money because we weren't old enough to be in the casino in the first place!

I have to give Stephanie credit, though. She's really a caring sister. I know she would do anything for me. When I was still going out with Steve, Stephanie overheard a conversation between Steve and this other girl. She was convinced Steve was cheating on me. So she and Kimmy broke into his apartment to find out the truth. Steve and I caught them there red-handed. Boy was I mad! But we talked about it later and I realized she only did it because she didn't want me to get hurt. Oh, by the way, Steve wasn't cheating on me. That other girl was his cousin.

You both look confused. Do you want me to repeat that? Sometimes I talk too fast and I...

Gambling . . . driving underage . . . breaking and entering . . .

Well, maybe I shouldn't have told you *those* stories. Stephanie really is an upstanding citizen. Honest! This won't jeopardize our winning the contest, will it?

Uh, no, I think it will be okay. She doesn't have a police record, does she?

Not yet. I mean no, she doesn't.

And what about your sister Michelle? She isn't headed for a life of crime, is she?

No way! Michelle is the best! Well, she *did* knock over an entire dinosaur skeleton once during a field trip to the museum, but it was only an accident and she didn't get arrested or anything.

That's good to hear.

Michelle was the baby in our family for a long time. Then my cousins Nicky and Alex were born. At first, Michelle had a hard time adjusting to all the attention being paid to the babies. And it didn't make it any easier when they were born right in the middle of her fifth birthday party. Everyone had to leave — well, of course we *all* had to take Aunt Becky to the hospital!

Now Michelle is kind of like a big sister to Nicky and Alex. As a matter of fact, she's the only one they'll listen to! Even though she tends to be a bit bossy with them — you know, ordering them to clean her room and make her bed, that sort of thing — they're still crazy about her. They really look up to her.

How old is Michelle?

She's eight, but acts more like she's eighteen sometimes.

Really? How so?

Well, she does and says things that are just so out there sometimes! She's very mature for her age. Last year, when she was seven, Michelle was the talk of the town when she stood up to the popular kiddie show star, Rigby the Rhino.

What did she do?

When the Rigby the Rhino doll she ordered wasn't anything like the TV commercial promised it would be,

Michelle marched down to the mall where Rigby was making an appearance. She led a group of kids in a big protest and demanded Rigby give them all their money back. And thanks to Michelle, that's what happened. Everyone got their money back *and* an apology from Rigby the Rhino.

Oh, and Michelle is also the reason our big, happy family is still together.

What do you mean?

Last year, this really rich guy offered to buy our house for a lot of money. At first, we were all psyched — Dad was psyched about the money and Steph and I were psyched to move to a bigger house. But then Uncle Jesse and Aunt Becky started talking about getting a place of their own. And Joey said that maybe it was time he went out on his own, too. Well, when Michelle realized that we all weren't going to be together anymore, she came up with a plan to sabotage the inspection of the house. It worked because Dad decided he didn't want to sell the house after all, if it meant breaking up the family. Everyone realized how lucky they are to have each other.

What about your uncle Jesse? Tell us about him.

My uncle Jesse defines the word "cool." You should have seen him when he first came to live with us! He was this real rough, tough guy, who only cared about rock and roll, Elvis, and his hair. He still cares about those things, but he isn't so rough and tough anymore.

Why are you laughing?

Oh, I'm sorry. It's just that I was remembering when Uncle Jesse first came to live with us. He paraded around the house with this real "I'm a macho, cool dude" attitude all the time. Then Stephanie and I caught him singing and dancing to "I'm a Little Teapot" with Michelle!

He's obviously softened up a bit since moving in with you.

Yes, definitely. Now I don't think twice when I see Uncle Jesse jumping rope with Michelle, or singing "Itsy Bitsy Spider" to the twins. He's become a real softie. Aunt Becky is responsible for that change in him, too.

How long have they been married?

Four years. Dad introduced them. Becky was Dad's co-host on *Wake Up, San Francisco* and he introduced them on a plane ride to Tahoe. Uncle Jesse fell instantly in love. He first kissed her under the mistletoe at the airport. We were all stranded there one Christmas because of bad weather. But Aunt Becky says she didn't realize she was in love with Uncle Jesse until the night of this big charity bachelor auction. Uncle Jesse, Dad, and Joey were each auctioning off a date with themselves. Anyway, Aunt Becky ended up outbidding all these other women and paying a lot of money for a date with Uncle Jesse just so no one else could have him! It was all very romantic.

Are you close to your uncle Jesse?

Very! He's the best uncle, ever. And a great friend, too. Always available with a hug, good advice, or some great hair-care tips. Uncle Jesse is our resident expert on hair. To him, hair is very serious stuff. Stephanie once accidentally cut off a huge chunk of his hair and he freaked. At Nicky's and Alex's first haircut, Aunt Becky had to keep him from grabbing the scissors away from the barber.

Uncle Jesse and I have had our share of, uh, misunderstandings, too. Like the time he caught me with a beer in my hand.

A beer?

It wasn't mine, I swear! And that's exactly what I told Uncle Jesse. The only reason I was holding a beer was to show some of the kids at school how stupid they looked while drinking. Uncle Jesse believed me and was pretty cool about it, but he did make me sit through an hour-long speech.

Honestly though, my uncle Jesse is one in a million. No other guy in the world (except maybe my dad) is such a good father to his kids. He and Aunt Becky don't always agree on how to raise Nicky and Alex, but they are really doing an excellent job. Those two kids are adorable. I remember when Uncle Jesse first found out that Aunt Becky was pregnant. Boy, did he freak out! He wasn't sure if he would make a good father. And then, when he found out Aunt Becky was having twins, he nearly fainted. But he's come a long way since then. He's really a super dad. Well, he *did* get the twins mixed up once when they were infants, but that was only for a few hours.

How did he finally tell them apart?

Aunt Becky was able to tell them apart by checking their footprints on their birth certificates.

Your aunt Becky...what's your relationship with her?

Aunt Becky is like a mother and a big sister all rolled into one. She's helped me get through everything — dates, school, my big breakup with Steve — everything.

Aunt Becky and I are so close that she sometimes get caught in the middle between trying to be my friend and my part-time mom. I remember once, when Kimmy and I secretly invited these guys over to the house where Kimmy was baby-sitting, and we told Aunt Becky about it. She promised not to tell Dad, but I messed up and stayed out longer than I was supposed to. When Dad asked Aunt Becky where I was, she had to tell him. I guess I'm glad though, because I would have felt terrible if Aunt Becky had to lie for me.

Were you —

Yes, I got grounded.

Uh, no, I wasn't going to ask that. But I'm sorry to hear it. I was going to ask if you were angry with your aunt for telling on you.

At first, yes. I felt as if she'd betrayed me. But I knew I was really to blame for everything. After all, Aunt Becky didn't do anything wrong.

How's your relationship now?

Aunt Becky is still always there for me. Just like she was there for me during a very hard time in junior high. My best friend, Kimmy, was having this pool party for her fourteenth birthday, and I didn't want to go. I was embarrassed to wear a bathing suit in front of my friends because I thought I looked fat. Anyway, I went on this crazy, stupid diet, where I practically starved myself, and then I went to the gym with my family.

You can probably guess what happened next. Right, I fainted from a lack of food. Right there in the gym, in front of everyone. I'm okay now, but thanks to Aunt Becky, I learned what I did was really wrong and very dumb. She told me that if I wanted to lose weight, I needed to eat sensibly. But more importantly, she convinced me that it's the person inside that counts most.

She sounds like a wonderful person, D.J. We'd like to know about this Joseph Gladstone you mentioned on your entry form. What is he, an uncle, a cousin?

Well, no, not exactly. Joey isn't related to me by blood, but he is family. I had to include Joey on the entry form. He's very special to me. To everyone.

Why is that?

Well, Joey is my dad's best friend since fifth grade. He came to live with us when Uncle Jesse did — right after my mom died. Ever since then, he's been just as much an uncle to me as my real uncle.

How so?

Joey always makes time for me. If I have a problem, or I'm sad, I almost always go to Joey first. Even before going to Dad. That's because Joey really knows how to cheer me up. He's super funny, so almost everything he says makes me laugh. And he does these hysterical cartoon voices that make me laugh even more. He helps me get through my problems and helps me see that sometimes laughter is the best medicine, as they say.

I remember once, a few years ago, Stephanie was feeling sad about not having a mother. So anyway, I sat Stephanie down for a sister-to-sister talk and told her this: "Steph," I said, "true, we don't have a mother, but we have something just as great. A terrific father, a great aunt and uncle, and a Joey. Now that's special. How many of your friends can say they have a Joey?"

It really made her feel better. She knows that our family wouldn't be as wonderful as it is without Joey. He's the most lovable guy we know. I really hope he falls in love and gets married soon. He'd make the greatest father. Ever since that first night when Joey was left in charge to baby-sit me, Steph, and Michelle, I've known he was "Great Dad Material." Actually, he grounded me that first night he baby-sat for us, so I take that back. Ever since the second night he baby-sat for us, I've known.

But honestly, you won't find a nicer guy. This is someone who left a good job in order to work at home and be close to his best friend's three daughters. This is someone who actually dressed up in Ninja Turtle pajamas and took Stephanie to her Honey Bees Mother/Daughter sleepover so she wouldn't feel left out. And this is someone who surprised me with a car on my sixteenth birthday. Okay, it was a used car and it fell apart on the day I got it — and it was *stolen* — but it was the thought that counted.

What does Joey do for a living?

He's a radio talk show host with my uncle Jesse. Their show is called *The Rush Hour Renegades* and it's great. Joey is a stand-up comedian. He went on *Star Search* and he even opened for Wayne Newton in Las Vegas. But he left the stand-up comedy business after landing a job hosting a kiddie television show as Ranger Joe.

Well, I have to be honest, D.J., the contest rules require all entrants to be related. I don't know if we can include Joseph in —

Oh, but you have to! Joey is one of the most important people in my life! I could never leave him out — it would be like leaving out my dad or my sisters.

Why is that?

You see, Joey is a parent to me in every sense of the word, except for the fact that we're not related. He loves me, he cares about me, he helped me grow up. There was this time I was mad at Dad for not letting me go on a study abroad trip to Spain. I was furious and refused to talk to him. Joey told me that because of a grudge he held against his own father, they didn't speak or see each other for years. Joey made me realize how important my family is to me. Because of Joey, I sat down and had a long talk with my dad and in the end, he agreed to send me to Spain because I'd showed him how mature I'd become.

I know Joey's not my real father, but fathers come in all types. Like if I was adopted, then I wouldn't actually be blood-related to my father, but he'd still be my father, right? Well, that's how it is with Joey. Think of Joey as my adopted, co-father.

I'm sure he'd be happy to hear how much you care about him.

You have to understand, Mr. Fabres, I have to include Joey. If I can't, then I might as well resign from this contest right now. There is no Tanner Family without Joey Gladstone.

You don't have to resign, D.J. You've convinced us to include Joey. He's obviously an important part of your family and of

your life. However, our time is almost up. We have to interview another entrant. Is there anything you'd like to add before we finish?

Yes. I just want to say that I'm happy and proud to be part of such a large family. People always ask me, "How can you live with so many people under one roof?" And it's true, there are times I'd like to move out — somewhere far, far, away where there isn't a soul for miles and I can talk on the phone for as long as I want, play the stereo as loud as I want, or date whomever I want. But mostly, I think having so many people around who love and care about me is the absolute best. And honestly, I'll be sad when the time comes for me to move out.

Thank you, D.J. It was a pleasure meeting you. We'll be notifying the winning family this Saturday night. Good luck!

•　　•　　•　　•　　•　　•

Man, that was tough! I was in there for close to an hour. I hope I answered all their questions correctly. They really got me nervous with all that stuff about not including Joey. And stupid me, I should never have told them all those Stephanie stories.

Funny, I could swear I just saw Stephanie coming out of the ladies' room down the hall. It looked just like her — same hair, same jeans, and same red high-tops. Oh, who am I kidding? Stephanie is way across town at dance class so it couldn't possibly have been her.

Anyway, it's over now. There's nothing else I can do except sit back and wait. Four days until Saturday.

Can I really keep my mouth shut that long?

STEPHANIE'S

FULL HOUSE

FLIP~OVER BOOK

STEPHANIE'S

FULL HOUSE

FLIP~OVER BOOK

By Devra Speregen

A Creative Media Applications Production

SCHOLASTIC INC.
New York Toronto London Auckland Sydney

ISBN 0-590-20257-X

TM & © 1994 Warner Bros. Television
All rights reserved. Published by Scholastic Inc.

12 11 10 9 8 7 6 5 4 3   4 5 6 7 8 9/9

Printed in the U.S.A.   40

First Scholastic printing, November 1994

STEPHANIE

What in the world could they be doing? I've been sitting here for forty-five minutes already! Boy, do I have to use the bathroom. I always have to go when I'm nervous.

Why are they taking so long? I'll bet the person they're interviewing right now is just like D.J. Going on and on and on about absolutely nothing.

Sheesh! Forty-*six* minutes!

I entered my family in this contest for Family of the Year. I filled out an entry form a couple of weeks ago, and they called me down here for an interview with their judges. I had to take two buses and the BART to get here, but I made it. I would have asked Dad or Joey for a ride, but, you see, I'm trying to keep this whole contest thing a secret. They think I'm at dance class today.

Keeping this a secret from my family has been pretty tough. I almost blew it a few times already. The worst was this morning. I was trying to get ready for this interview, but I didn't have anything cool to wear. Luckily D.J. took

an extra-long shower and I was able to sneak her black bodysuit out of her closet.

I heard about the contest while I was shopping with Joey and Michelle a few weeks ago. Joey promised my dad he would take Michelle for new shoes, but we spent an hour in the video arcade playing Space Mutant Warriors instead and the shoe store closed.

Anyway, Michelle and Joey were involved in an intense game, so I sneaked out of the arcade for some French fries. (Joey was supposed to take us to dinner, too.) That's when I saw the poster for the contest on the wall at Burger Barn. When I read it, I nearly squirted ketchup all over my shirt. It said there was a contest for "Golden Gate's Big, Happy Family of the Year."

Now does *my* family qualify for that or what? We're big! We're happy!

So I took an entry form from the display and filled it out while I ate my fries. I mailed it in a few days later, then I got this phone call a couple of days ago. Uncle Jesse answered the phone. He watched me suspiciously the entire time I spoke. I barely heard the guy on the phone,

Mr. Fabres, when he asked me to come in for an interview. After I hung up, I had to tell Uncle Jesse that Mr. Fabres was my health teacher. I hope he bought it.

It would be totally cool if we won. The Grand Prize is great — a big shopping spree, a family portrait, and an appearance on that TV show, *San Francisco Beat*. Going on TV would be pretty cool. I was on TV once before, but it was WUSF, my dad's network telethon. I danced, but not too many people saw it.

Wow, they're still in there! I can't believe it. What could possibly be taking so long? This is making me incredibly nervous. And when I get nervous — well, you know. I can't hold it in any longer. I'm going to the bathroom.

They'll probably still be in there when I get back anyway.

• • • • • •

Big, Happy

Family of the Year

OFFICIAL CONTESTANT ENTRY FORM

Contestant Family: __The Tanner Family__

Name of Applicant: __Stephanie Tanner__

Address: __1882 Girard Street__
__San Francisco, California__

CONTESTANT FAMILY

Please list all family members, their occupations, and relationship to applicant.

Name	Occupation	Relationship
1. Stephanie Tanner	Baby-sitter/ Student	Me
2. Danny Tanner	TV Star	My Dad
3. D.J. Tanner	High School Student + Smash Club Waitress	My Sister
4. Michelle Tanner	Dog Walker/ Kid	My Sister
5. Jesse Katsopolis	Rocker/ Radio Star + Smash Club Owner	My Uncle

Hey! How come there's only five spaces?
I thought this was an entry form
for a BIG family! Five
isn't big at all.

Rebecca Donaldson Katsopolis	TV Star	My Aunt
Nicky Katsopolis	Toddler	My Cousin
Alex Katsopolis	Toddler	My Cousin
Joey Gladstone	TV and Radio Star	My Joey
Comet Tanner	Dog	Family Dog

APPLICANT'S PERSONAL INFORMATION

Name: **Stephanie Tanner**

Hair color: **Blond**

Eye color: **Blue**

Level of education: **I'm in the seventh grade.**

PLEASE ANSWER THE FOLLOWING QUESTIONS ABOUT YOUR

FAMILY TO THE BEST OF YOUR ABILITY.

1. Why do you feel your family should be nominated as Golden Gate's Big, Happy Family of the Year? **We're definitely a BIG family. Everyone says so. And we're pretty ~~hra~~ happy, most of the time. But I'd have to say it's because we all help each other out so much. In my house, everybody helps out. We take turns with the**

dishes, we take turns babysitting and we take turns doing the shopping. Last year, Uncle Jesse bought the Smash Club and we all helped out when it opened. D.J. was a waitress and Michelle and I were customers. Joey was supposed to book R.E.M. to play at the opening, but he goofed and hired Renee, Esther, and Martha instead. It was still fun though. And when Michelle thought she lost her bike a few months ago, everybody pitched in to help her find it. Only she didn't really lose it, she left it at her friend's house.

2. What exciting things does your family do together? We throw great parties. People always say our parties are the coolest. We've had birthday parties for me, Michelle, and D.J., a surprise 26th birthday party for Uncle Jesse, a Christmas party, and we even had a 60th Wedding Anniversary party for Uncle Jesse's grandparents, Iorgos and Gina. They flew in from Greece for the party and it was wild! There was dancing and singing ... even plate smashing! When D.J. graduated junior high the same time Michelle graduated preschool, Joey threw a party for me — I was going into fourth grade — just so I wouldn't feel left out. I threw our dog,

Comet, a first birthday party and invited all the neighborhood dogs. It was so funny, I had a little cake for him with seven candles for one dog year.

But the most exciting event was Uncle Jesse's and Aunt Becky's wedding. I'm talking total fun. Uncle Jesse disappeared the morning before the wedding to have one last adventure before getting hitched. But he ended up getting stuck in a tree after parachuting out of a plane! Then he stole a truck to get to the church for the wedding, but he got arrested on the way and Aunt Becky had to bail him out of jail in her wedding dress.

STEPHANIE • 13

Boy, you ~~really~~ don't give a lot of space for these answers. Anyway, they finally got a ride back to the church on a bus full of choir singers and had a really beautiful wedding. I was a bridesmaid with D.J. and Michelle was the flower girl. We had an awesome party back at our house afterward, and threw rice at Uncle Jesse and Aunt Becky as they rode off on a motorcycle!

3. How do the members of your family get along? __We get__ __along great.__ My older sister, D.J., can be really moody sometimes, like when she broke up with her boyfriend, Steve, last year and moped around for days, but she's usually pretty fun. I live with Michelle, my younger sister now. We share a room. Me and Deej used to share a room, but she moved out on me. (She said it was a privacy thing.) Michelle's a pretty good roommate, but when she first moved in, I had to set her straight. I told her absolutely no dopey pink teddy-bear pictures on the wall. We get along great now, though I should never have taught her

how to tap dance. What was I thinking? Dad and Joey and Uncle Jesse get along great, too. Dad was mad at Uncle Jesse when he asked Joey to be his best man, but then Uncle Jesse asked him, too, and everything was all right again.

4. What makes your family big and happy? **We're not really _that_ big, you know. There's this family down the block with seven kids, two dogs, and a cat. Now that's _big_. But we're much happier than they are. Lots of things make me happy. Dancing especially. My dance teacher said I have what it takes to be a professional dancer. But I didn't want to practice twenty-four hours a day, every day, for the rest of my life, so I decided not to do it. I wanted to be able to go on family vacations and to Aunt Becky's baby shower instead. Boys make D.J. happy. And privacy. She's always whining**

about how happy she would be
if she had more privacy.
Cleaning makes my dad happy.
Scrubbing and waxing in
particular.   Joey says the girl
who works at the Fotomat
makes him very happy. And
Uncle Jesse and Aunt Becky say
the twins make them the
happiest they've ever been in
their lives.   Michelle is easy.
Anything with chocolate makes
her happy.

5. List three good things about having a big, happy family:

1) There's always someone to talk to.

2) Cool hand-me-downs!

3)

and three bad things:

1) We're always out of toilet paper.

2) It's impossible to keep a secret.

3) There's never enough moo shoo pork to go around.

STEPHANIE

The Interview

Oh, there you are, Stephanie. We thought you didn't show up. Nice to meet you. Sorry to have kept you waiting so long.

No problem, really. Lovely offices you have here. I was just, uh, taking a tour of this fine establishment. Lovely. And the bathroom. It's lovely, too.

Oh, well, thank you. Please, have a seat. My name is Michael Fabres and this is Shirley Newman. We only want to talk to you a little bit about your family. Get to know you. That type of thing. So don't be nervous.

Nervous? Who me? Ha! I'm never nervous. (Yeah, right. I'm practically shaking in my shoes. Don't blow this, Tanner! Wait! I know! Open with a funny story! That's what Joey always says to do when you're nervous about speaking in front of people.)

So let us start by asking you —

Can I tell you something my little sister did this last week that was hilarious?

Uh, well, actually we're supposed to ask the questions, Stephanie.

Oh, right. Sorry. Okay, ask away.

Well, since you brought it up, why don't you tell us what your little sister did last week.

Sure, no problem. It was really funny. You see, Michelle is eight years old, and very . . . um, *outspoken*. Whatever is on her mind usually comes flying right out of her mouth. So anyway, Uncle Jesse, Michelle, and I were waiting for a bus to the supermarket last week and there was this pregnant woman waiting at the bus stop with us. Michelle kept looking up at her stomach — she was huge. Finally, the bus came and we got on and there were only three seats left. So Michelle, in a loud voice, tells her, "You should sit here, lady. So in case you have the baby on the

bus, my uncle Jesse can help you push and breathe."

Isn't that funny? You see, my aunt Rebecca had twins a few years ago and, well, I guess you had to be there.

Michelle is your younger sister, right?

Yes. She's eight.

Oh, yes, it says that right here on your entry form. It was covered by a big smudge. Ketchup, I think. Anyway, she's some character, your sister Michelle, isn't she?

Oh, yeah. Michelle always says something crazy like that — ever since she learned to talk. In fact, I think her first words were, "Move it, Buster!"

How do you get along with Michelle?

How do I get along with Michelle? Are you writing this down? Okay, then put down that we get along great. No, make that nicely. That we get along nicely.

Michelle is pretty easy to get along with. All you need is a plate of cookies or brownies and you can get her to do

whatever you want. Sometimes she's a real pest, though. I remember one time she followed me around the house for a whole week, copying me and repeating whatever I said. It drove me nuts! She said she was playing something called the Shadow Game. All I know is I wanted to tape her mouth shut.

But when she's not being pesty, Michelle can be incredibly sweet. She did this really cool thing for me once, and I'll never forget it. We were at Disney World on one of our Tanner Family Vacations. It was a great trip, up until Michelle was picked as "Princess for the Day." I was so bummed — I was hoping to be the Princess.

Anyway, as Princess, Michelle was able to have anything she wished for. So when she saw how unhappy I was, she wished that I could be Princess, too. We both got to ride in the Princess float in the Main Street Parade.

What about your other sister, D.J.?

What about her?

Are you as close to her?

Oh, yeah, definitely. Me and Deej go way back. We've been sisters for thirteen years, you know.

D.J. is the best big sister a girl could ask for. She *is* smart, pretty, and she gives me advice about boys. Not always good advice, I might add.

What do you mean?

Well, there was this one time when my friend Josh from softball and I went out for pizza with D.J. and her ex-boyfriend, Steve. D.J. and her dopey friend Kimmy Gibbler kept calling it a date and they got me all nervous. Meanwhile, we were just two teammates going out for pizza! So I asked D.J. what I should do, and she told me that if I like him, I should show him. Well, I was so crazy thinking about this date thing, I ended up kissing him. "What did you do that for?" he asked me. It was humiliating. It's a good thing Josh didn't slug me, though I wished I could have slugged D.J.

Anyway, I think D.J. is just plain boy-crazy. You should see her when she falls for a guy. It's like she's walking

around in a fog. Like the time when she was first going out with Steve — it was like no one else existed! It got so bad, do you know what happened? I'll tell you. Then you'll see how spacey my sister can be sometimes. It was when Dad wouldn't let her go to Steve's new apartment because she missed her curfew one night. So she and Steve hadn't seen each other for, what, about twenty minutes? Anyway, Steve came over and they ran into the backyard to smooch. Only they needed super-duper privacy and decided to kiss in the cement truck that was back there. (Uncle Jesse and Joey were putting in a new driveway.) Anyway, D.J. and Steve were so lost in their own little world, they accidentally bumped into a switch and poured wet cement through our kitchen window!

The . . . *kitchen*?

Yeah, can you believe that! The kitchen was completely ruined. It was some mess. I, for one, would never let something like that happen.

I see.

But D.J. has a history of this sort of stuff — I don't know what it is about that sister of mine, but accidents seem to happen around her. Maybe it's because she's always hanging around with that string bean troublemaker, Kimmy Gibbler. Gibbler is trouble with a capital T. Not only that, she's such a dope, she has to tie a string around her finger to remind her that there are strings around her finger to remember to do things.

Kimmy Gibbler? I don't see her name on your application. Is she a relative?

A relative? Yikes! No way! Don't even joke about that. Actually, Gibbler did live in our house once for two whole days. It was when D.J. had this assignment from school to write a paper on what it's like to be another person. She chose Kimmy. So she switched places with Gibbler and that annoying girl took over our house and ruined my life for forty-eight hours. I had to stuff cotton in my ears to keep from going bonkers. It was my worst nightmare come true.

So tell us more about your father. If you could describe him in just one word, what would it be?

Neat. And I mean that two ways. Neat as in cool. And neat as in clean, spotless, dust-free. My dad is the co-host of *Wake Up, San Francisco*. Maybe you've seen him? He's the one who's always wiping off his coffee mug when the camera comes back from a commercial. He says it's his signature thing. Maybe someday he'll be famous for it.

I don't watch very much television. But go on.

Dad's totally obsessed with cleanliness. Would you believe he used to follow me to kindergarten —

And disinfect your nap mat?

Yes! Wow, how did you know that?

I had a hunch.

That's amazing. Anyway, once, on Tanner Family Clean-up Day, Dad made us all stay inside and clean, even

though it was a gorgeous day out. Everyone was grumpy and moaning except for Dad. He whistled away, polishing the silver and waxing the kitchen floor. But then we started complaining about Dad, and the way he's so crazy about cleaning. He happened to be in a closet at the time. He was polishing his shoe trees. Anyway, he heard every word and was pretty upset by what we'd said. So he decided to change his ways and live life as a slob. He threw junk on the floor, put his feet up on the table — I tell you, we didn't recognize him. All I can say is that when it was all over, I was glad to have my clean, spotless, dust-free dad back again.

How would you describe your relationship with your father?

The perfect Father/Daughter relationship. I don't get grounded nearly as much as D.J. so I don't have too many complaints about Dad. He's actually a really cool dad, for someone who works on a local television station.

Dad always comes up with the greatest surprises. On my tenth birthday, he arranged for this really hot singing teen idol to come to my party! Dad knew I had a huge

crush on him so he set up the whole thing. Wasn't that nice of him?

Sometimes though, my dad goes overboard. Like the time I won my class spelling bee and was asked to compete in the fourth-grade finals. I asked Dad to help me study and he went totally crazy, buying like ten different dictionaries and making all these word lists and stuff. He even woke me up in the middle of the night and asked me to spell words. He kept telling me over and over that to help me remember how to spell words, I should use mnemonic devices, like if you're trying to remember all the Great Lakes, you just have to think of the word HOMES. That stands for Huron, Ontario, Michigan, Erie, and Superior. HOMES is a mnemonic device. Anyway, he kept yelling "Mnemonic devices! Mnemonic devices!" at me for a week, beating it into my brain. And guess what happened? My first word to spell in the competition was "mnemonic" and I choked.

But I know he does it all because he's proud of me. Aside from the fact that he's overly enthusiastic sometimes, he really is a great father. Last year, when I

had this problem with some new kids I met in junior high, he gave me great advice.

What was the problem?

These seventh–grade girls I met in the school bathroom were smoking and they wanted me to be in their clique. I hate smoking, but I really wanted to make some new friends. It was obvious that if I didn't smoke, I wouldn't be accepted into the "cool" group. Dad said that a true friend wouldn't make me do anything I wouldn't want to do. He was right about that. One of the girls, Mickey, stopped hanging around with those other kids and she and I became great friends. She quit smoking, too.

Your father is a smart man. Is Uncle Jesse your father's brother?

No, he's my mom's brother. My mother died when I was little and my uncle Jesse came to live with us to help my father take care of us. Then he met Aunt Becky and they got married. And then they had Nicky and Alex.

Uncle Jesse and Aunt Becky are great. My friends are always jealous when they meet them because they are just so cool. I have to admit I was a little jealous when the twins were born and they got all Aunt Becky's and Uncle Jesse's attention, but I'm over it now. I had Uncle Jesse for seven years so now Nicky and Alex have their chance. And besides, I'm much more grown-up now and I can handle my problems on my own. Most of them, anyway.

When the twins were first born, they didn't do very much except sleep, eat, and cry, but now they're three years old and into everything! My aunt and uncle are usually exhausted, so I like to help them out by baby-sitting for the boys. I first baby-sat for them when they started crawling. Well, actually, Kimmy was the official baby-sitter then because Uncle Jesse thought I was too young for the job. Meanwhile, Gibbler sat on her skinny butt all night and I did all the work.

What was it like having Uncle Jesse in the house while you were growing up?

Fun! He always wore a black leather jacket and looked so

cool. And that hair! Uncle Jesse doesn't know the true meaning of a "bad hair day." Wait, I take that back. When I was like six or seven, I accidentally cut off a teeny-tiny, itsy-bitsy piece of his hair. He freaked. I think that was a bad hair day for him.

Is he your role model?

Yes. Dad, Joey, and Uncle Jesse are perfect role models. I'm very proud of my uncle Jesse. When we all learned that he never graduated high school, we encouraged him to go back and finish. He was nervous, but he finally went to night school and got his diploma. That took a lot of guts.

What about you and your aunt Becky?

I'm really close to my aunt Becky, too. We have girl talks all the time — I usually go to her for advice when D.J. isn't around, or if we're not speaking, which, uh, doesn't happen very often like I mentioned before. Can I ask you something?

Sure.

Telling you about the fights and some of the bad things...will that ruin our chances of winning?

No. Don't worry about it. You were saying about your aunt Becky —

Right. Anyway, once, when I ACCIDENTALLY did something to our kitchen —I won't go into detail, but it was pretty bad — I ran away to Aunt Becky's apartment. I was much, much younger then and she and Uncle Jesse weren't married yet. Aunt Becky made me realize that no matter what I do, my dad will always love me. Even if I did something as bad as drive Joey's car through the kitchen. Whoops! I didn't mean to tell you that. Cross that out! Forget I mentioned it, okay?

Okay.

It wasn't really that bad anyway, just a tiny hole through the wall. Though if you ask D.J., she makes it sound as if I crashed the entire house down. Anyway, I forgot to tell

you that Uncle Jesse is in a rock band called Jesse and the Rippers. They are so good they made a record and toured in Japan! But Uncle Jesse quit the tour to spend more time with his family.

And what does he do now?

He owns the Smash Club and he's the host of a radio show with Joey. Uncle Jesse and Joey always end up working together. First they worked in an advertising company together. Then they formed their own advertising company and wrote jingles for commercials. And then, Uncle Jesse joined Joey's Ranger Joe show as Lumberjack Jess, but that didn't last very long. Uncle Jesse wasn't cut out to wear that dorky costume. He said that costume was meant more for someone named Hermes.

Hermes?

Yeah, that's Uncle Jesse's real name. He changed it when he was younger because he was embarrassed. I tease him about it all the — wait! Don't write that down! He'll kill me if he knew I told you. Please, cross that out, too.

I won't say a thing.

Thank you. Uncle Jesse would go totally crazy if he ever found out I said anything. Like the time I told Aunt Becky that Uncle Jesse sleeps with a picture of Elvis Presley under his pillow. They were only dating at the time and boy, did he flip.

No problem. We won't say a word. So, tell us about this "Joey" you keep mentioning.

Oh, that's Joey Gladstone. He's my...my...he's my Joey. I don't know how else to describe him. Joey is a very special person in my life. He also came to live in our house after my mom died. I guess he figured my dad needed all the help he could get.

From the very beginning, Joey and I hit it off. Maybe it's because we both have a great sense of humor. Of course, Joey is much, much funnier than I am. He's the funniest person I know! Now he is a stand-up comedian, and a sit-down comedian on the radio.

Did you know that Joey once broke my nose? No, of course you wouldn't know that. How could you? You

don't even know him. But he didn't do it on purpose. It happened when I was about nine. Joey was hosting *The Mr. Egghead Show* on TV, and he used me as his assistant to perform science tricks. Anyway, one of the tricks backfired and he accidentally broke my nose while we were on the air. It happened the same week I was having my class picture taken, so that was kind of a bummer. But I forgave him.

That was kind of you.

Well it didn't really hurt too much and, after all, Joey always does such great things for me it's hard to stay mad at him.

Want to know the greatest thing Joey ever did for me?

Sure.

When I was ten and Aunt Becky's car broke down on the night of the Honey Bees Mother/Daughter sleepover, Joey offered to take me. I have to admit I was a little embarrassed — especially when he wore those stupid

Ninja Turtle pajamas in front of all my friends and their moms — but I knew he was doing it all for me. He knew how sad I was that I didn't have a mother. His going to the sleepover meant a lot to me and I'll never forget it.

Joey has always been like a parent to me. After the big earthquake a couple of years ago, he sat up with me every night for a week when I was having bad dreams. And he comes to school with me on the first day every year so I don't get nervous. He even came with me this year, and I'm in the eighth grade.

He sounds very special.

He's a real cool guy. Everyone says that about him. Even people we meet for a few minutes at the deli counter. Joey once talked the deli lady into giving us a whole pound of free potato salad. She said he was "irresistable."

Joey's even on the P.T.A.! It's true. Last year he ran for president of the P.T.A. after he learned they were cutting the art program from Michelle's school. It was a wild election — Joey even managed to get Little Richard to play at his campaign rally. But later, when his opponent

claimed Joey wasn't eligible to run for president because he wasn't really a parent, Joey made this really terrific speech about what it means to be a parent. I swear, there wasn't a dry eye in the house. Even his opponent thought it was great and they were both elected co-presidents.

Basically, what I'm trying to say is that I couldn't love Joey any more if he were my own father. But he's not my father. He's my Joey.

Stephanie, we've really enjoyed hearing all about your family. Is there anything you would like to add before we end the interview?

Let me think. Oh, yeah, write this down. I want to add that I think the Tanners should win because they are the biggest, happiest family around. And if we do win, I promise to donate all the prize money to charity!

Well, that's very nice, Stephanie, but there is no prize money.

Oh, right. Well then, I promise that if we win, we won't disappoint San Francisco. All of us — Me, Dad, D.J.,

Michelle, Aunt Becky and Uncle Jesse, the twins, Joey, and even Comet, will live up to the title of Golden Gate's Big, Happy Family of the Year. We'll make San Francisco proud. And who knows? From there, maybe we'll enter California's Family of the Year Contest! And then America's Family of the Year! And maybe we Tanners will someday be named Earth's Big, Happy Family of the Year! Wow, wouldn't that be something?

Oh, and just so I know, are dogs included in that prize package shopping spree and family portrait?

• • • • • •

It's over! Whew, what a relief. Boy they were certainly a pair of tough cookies. That Newman lady didn't even crack a smile when I told her about Michelle and the pregnant lady. And Mr. Fabres never did answer me about dogs being in the portrait. It's a legitimate question. After all, Comet *is* a part of our family. He'd be pretty depressed if he couldn't be in the picture.

Anyway, I'd better get home and get this black

bodysuit back in D.J.'s closet. She'll kill me if she sees me wearing it.

Boy, I hope we win.

Saturday seems so far away.

This is a public service message for all Bay Area residents. My name is Michael Fabres and I am the president of the Golden Gate Special Events Organization. I'm proud to announce that we have chosen this year's Golden Gate Big, Happy Family of the Year!

I have to say, it was a very close race this year, but we were finally able to narrow it down to three families — the Carnes family from Berkeley, the Parker family from Sausalito, and the Tanner family from San Francisco. And moments ago, a final vote was taken among the judges in our organization and the Big, Happy Family of the Year has been chosen!

The winning family's name is written below in code. To find out who will be named this year's Golden Gate Big, Happy Family of the Year, write the letter of the alphabet that comes before each letter in the code name below. Then unscramble your answer.

GOLDEN GATE'S
Big, Happy Family of the Year

THE **SOFBOU** FAMILY !!!!!

THE _ _ _ _ _ _ FAMILY !!!!!